DAWN HUNTERS AND OTHER POEMS

ESCOPETISTAS DE LA AURORA Y OTROS POEMAS

Poems by
ROBERTO RIVERA-REYES

Translated by
Dinah Livingstone
Mike Baynham
Ana María Crowe Serrano

Latin American Writers Publication

First published in Great Britain by Latin American Writers Publication,
107 Gorefield House, Gorefield Place, London, NW6 5TB

Printed in Great Britain by Short Run Press 0296 631075

Cover illustration by Sergio Navarro 1989

Typeset by Boldface 01-253 2014 London, EC1

ISBN 1 871982 01 4

ROBERTO RIVERA-REYES

Roberto Rivera-Reyes was born in the Chilean capital Santiago and he has been writing since 1967. He studied Philosophy at the University of Chile, and he was involved in community cultural work there. His literary background was based on his participation in the two main literary workshops in Santiago, at the Andrés Bello Cultural Centre and at the Ministry of Education Cultural House during the Salvador Allende Government.

He went into exile after the military coup of General Pinochet. He spent some time in Colombia where he taught Social Sciences at the University Institute ITUSCO.

In September 1975, he was given refuge in Britain. Here he obtained a B.A. (Hons.) in Latin American Studies at Portsmouth Polytechnic and a P.G.C.E. at Cardiff University. He teaches languages in London.

In 1984, he was one of the founders of the Latin American Writers Group in London. He has read his poetry in several places throughout the country and, recently, he has read at the Almeida Theatre and in the Second International Poetry Festival in London, (1989).

He was the editor of the *Anthology of Latin American Poets in London*, (London, 1988). A selection of his poems have been published in several literary publications such as *Westwords* (Autumn, 1987), *Artrage* (London, March, 1986), *Ampersand* (Cambridge, 1985 No 5), *Publishing for People and Fighting Censorship* (Anthology, London, 1985) and *Epigramas de Harina Neruda* (London, 1983).

CONTENTS

Dinah Livingstone's latest collection is *Keeping Heart Poems 1967-89* (1989), covering the period she has lived in Camden Town, London. She has given many performances of her work at home and abroad and Roberto Rivera translated some of her poems into Spanish for her reading at the Rubén Darío Festival in Nicaragua in 1988.

Some of the Latin American works she has translated are: Ernesto Cardenal, *Love* (1974); Helder Camara, *The Desert is Fertile* (1974); A. Pérez Esclarin, *Jesus of Gramoven* (novel, 1980); Carlos Mejía Godoy, *Nicaraguan Mass* (songs, 1986); Anthology of Latin American Poets in London (part, 1988); Ernesto Cardenal *Nicaraguan New Time* (poems, 1988); C. and L.E. Mejía Godoy and Julio Valle-Castillo, *The Nicaraguan Epic* (songs and poems, 1989).

INTRODUCTION

Roberto Rivera-Reyes was forced into exile as a result of the 1973 coup in Chile when General Pinochet overthrew the elected socialist government of Salvador Allende. When their lives were endangered Roberto and his wife Hilda took refuge in the Colombian embassy. They spent some time in Colombia and finally arrived in Britain in September 1975.

All the poems in this collection were written since the coup, those up to and including *The Murdered Defence* in Chile and Colombia, *Origins* was begun in Colombia and finished in Britain and the rest were written here. After fourteen years, Roberto has become one of the chief exiled Chilean poets writing in Britain and has given many performances of his work. He has a voice with a metallic quality to it and rather a delicate and sallow dark presence. The performance style is both formal and very intense, sometimes almost keening the poems, which has the paradoxical effect of externalising them from himself, while at the same time increasing their emotional charge.

He writes a severely traumatised poetry in which the themes of violence and exile constantly recur in language varying from lucid and lyrical to convoluted, florid and at times bombastic. The book begins with a haunting poem for the disappeared, *Black-necked Swan*, who searches the lake for prisoners that are not found:

> That's why they say
> that All Saints' Lake
> now has a fathomless
> floor of lost faces.

The persistent theme of sterility and waste occurs here for the first time:

Wet-dreamlike
dripped from inside you
a white drop of hope
rolling away
in a desperate flight
and seeking.

Resisting fascist force is an 'apocalyptic flower' which grew on the railway and day after day 'stood against God in his iron passing'.

Demented Dreams, the first of the poems written in Britain, describes exile as a sea voyage, from which you may never land again. Corpses are washed up on board and in the gothic-horror ending, which nevertheless convinces as an exile metaphor, the protagonist 'refuses his irreversible solitude' and tries to revive the corpse by making love to her:

He sank into her
with his blind heart on fire
till her cold silence burst it.
The ship sailed on and was lost in mist.

Here the heart is broken but the theme of resistance recurs all through the book as a refusal to accept defeat in poems such as *So Let's Live*:

Revolutionary power
which resists being shot down . . .
we want to be butterfly chrysalis-freed,
triumphant spring with blossoms and garlands,
dance the love waltz in the El Sol carnival.

One way resistance is expressed is in the primal forest poems such as *The Earth Must Stay Free Forever*, in which the forest itself defeats the conquistadors:

There colonising exploiting conquistadors
were swallowed by earth forever.
Trees swallowed them through their roots,
because the earth must stay free forever.

Roberto is of Spanish descent himself but, as a victim of a new tyranny in Chile, identifies with the Indians, particularly the Mapuche, who resisted the conquistadors for two hundred years. Two difficult but powerful recent poems, the title poem, *Dawn Hunters* and *Millarai*, interlock the Indians' fight against the conquistadors with resistance to fascism today. The Indians represent a view of humanity in harmony with nature, that treats the planet with respect, a feeling which also energises other lyrical and mysterious forest poems, such as *Forest Epitaphs* and *The Voice of the Wood*.

Later the theme is universalised in the anti-nuclear poem *Don Quixote's Windmills*, in which Don Quixote, with a gas mask as the crest of his heraldic insignia, rides again to defend the planet against wanton destruction.

It is admirable that Roberto in this and other more recent poems has moved outwards beyond himself to embrace the rest of humanity and our planet. His poems clearly – also quite often obscurely, sometimes even with a sense of demented ranting – convey in image after image the deep psychic damage done by the experience of fascism and exile. In the poem *Michael Dolan's Spring* about a Scottish teaching colleague's suicide, Roberto's own pain has enabled him to feel with his subject from the inside and gives this lament its peculiar power, as 'bagpipes in the night lament you, Michael Dolan.' This also happens in *Stone Orange*, his poem for Palestine.

Erich Fried, a Jewish exile from Nazi-occupied Vienna, also gave strong support to Palestine's aspirations and Roberto expresses what is perhaps his own ideal of humanity in his poem for Erich Fried, written just after Erich's recent death:

Insistent and deep
your socialist humanist voice
speaks to dolphins
young holocaust orphans.
Unfenced is this love's field,
'it is what is' . . .
your smile wanting to get things done.

He praises Erich as 'a contemporary saint, a revolutionary':

Chile will feel your silence
when she is rid of fascism,
then Erich Fried, the voices of Chile,
Nicaragua, Palestine
will be calling for you to come
back down to our earth
crying: We need
Freedom!

In *Annunciation*, the last poem in the book, Roberto recalls the violence, pain, damage and exile but his final assertion defies them all:

If to love you I must die
I'll give you back your white lilies
and give back your challenge:
to love I shall live.

His poetry forms an extreme contrast with the poetry now being written in Nicaragua, where shortly after the Sandinista victory of 1979, graffiti on a wall in León rapturously proclaimed: 'The Triumph of the Revolution is the Triumph of Poetry.'

Roberto's poetry can nag like a toothache, pound like hailstones, forbid with its verbosity but is nevertheless compelling. It is the genuine voice of exiled Chile. It is also a voice that has refused to let the handicap of exile become an excuse for narcissism (and it is not difficult for a poet in Britain's present climate to be self-absorbed and 'privatised' without that excuse). Particularly in the more recent poems, which lead us to think this is a course that will continue, Roberto's voice has begun reaching out to the rest of the world. As the voice matures, it grows in awareness that as individuals, whose language and physical membership of one another make us by nature social beings, and *as* a species, human is something we need to become.

Dinah Livingstone
May 1989

ACKNOWLEDGMENTS

The present volume contains translations of twenty-five poems by Roberto Rivera-Reyes. The poems were selected, and arranged in the order in which they appear in the book by the author.

I should like to thank to the translators Dinah Livingstone, Mike Baynham and Ana María Crowe Serrano, who kindly helped me and made it possible for these poems to be accessible to a wider readership.

My affectionate thanks to Dinah from whom I have received invaluable support throughout these years we have worked together.

My special thanks to Sergio Navarro, Ciaran Cosgrove, Hilda Kaune and Auristela Reyes Olguin for their encouragement and moral support.

RRR

POEMS

CISNE DE CUELLO NEGRO
(En busca de los prisioneros que no aparecen)

Fría es la aurora
sin la luna
amada mía,
sin la luz
que te ilumine,
sin sus ojos
que te sigan.

Oscura es la noche
sin la luna
amada mía,
cuando se va sola
entre la negra espuma
buscando la sangre vertida.

Hay que encontrar
esa copa de sangre
amada mía,
el crisol de los hornos profundos,
para derretir la sustancia de los muertos,
que yacen en estas aguas sin horizontes
del Lago de Todos los Santos.

La noche sin luna
amada mía,
ató a tu cuello de cisne
una pregunta desgarradora.
Es un rosario de mandas
hecho de espinas rosas
que cuelga de tu cuello enlutado,
y se enredó en tus volcanes lácteos
que amamantan al niño ausente.

BLACK-NECKED SWAN
(searching for prisoners who are not found)

Cold is the dawn
with no moon,
my love,
with no light
to light you,
without its eyes
to pursue you.

Dark is the night
with no moon,
my love,
sailing alone
through black ripples
searching for blood that was spilt.

This cup of blood
must be found,
my love,
crucible to consume
the substance of the dead
abed in unbounded waters
of All Saints' Lake.

The moonless night,
my love,
hung on the question-mark
of your black swan-neck
a rosary of requests
woven of briar rose brambles
from tangles on milky volcanoes,
that had suckled a child now gone.

Los pechos fructíferos
buscan la boca inocente
con sus labios de fuego.
Que les beba de sus ojos
un deseo de sangre
con la fuerza del hambre.

Y como en un sueño nocturno,
de tus entrañas se desprendió
una gota alba,
de espera,
que roda
en un desesperado acto de fuga
y de búsqueda.

Espesa y profunda
es el agua oscura
amada mía,
allí donde el alma desaparece,
donde van a caer las estrellas
que se disipan en la noche.
Por eso dicen
que el Lago de Todos los Santos
ya no tiene fondo
de tantas miradas ocultas.

Heavy breasts
press to innocent mouths
and their lips' longing.
Let desire in the blood
drink from eyes
hungrily.

Wet-dreamlike
dripped from inside you
a white drop of hope
rolling away
in a desperate flight
and seeking.

Thick and deep
is the dark water,
my love,
where souls disappear,
stars fall
and fade in the night.
That's why they say
that All Saints' Lake
now has a fathomless
floor of lost faces.

D.L.

LLUEVE EN TI Y SE POR QUE

Salar de lágrimas
mar de llantos

Lagunilla de ojos tristes,
estrella solitaria de los ríos
y de los grandes mares embravecidos.

Maquinaria de destinos quebrados,
bala arcaica.

WEEP AND KNOW WHY

Salt pool of tears,
sea of lamentation.
Bitterly fill deep pits,
eyes weep desolate.

Solitary star of rivers
and gigantic angry ocean.
Machinery of shattered fates,
archaic cannon shot.

D.L.

FLOR APOCALIPTICA

Nacida en vía férrea
flor apocalíptica,
que día a día
resistes a Dios
al paso del fierro.

Naciste con alma foliácea
de viento otoñal,
húmeda por el rocío crepuscular
y parecieras flotar
en tu atmósfera de congoja.

En cada aurora apareciste flotando
en la rivera del río Mapocho,
trayendo contigo cuerpos albos
desnudos de vida.

APOCALYPTIC FLOWER

On the railway you grew,
apocalyptic flower.
Day in day out
you stood against God
in his iron passing.

Your leafy spirit
sprang gusty autumnal,
drank evening dew.
Now you seem to hover
in your air of sadness.

Each dawn you float
on the waters
of the River Mapocho
along with pale bodies,
stripped lifeless.

D.L.

Santiago, the capital of Chile, stands on the River Mapocho. Immediately after Pinochet's coup d'état dead bodies were seen floating in the river every day.

APOLOGIA ASESINADA

THE MURDERED DEFENCE

APOLOGIA ASESINADA 1

Han venido a clavar sus banderas de exterminio
a nuestra tierra germinada.
Han venido a entristecer nuestro cielo
con sus puertas de cementerios
y sus ventanas carcelarias.
Han venido a clavar en ella,
la ley de sus perros obscenos,
tediosos en vanidad del Culebrón,
que va apuñalando,
estrangulando y exprimiendo
el trabajo obrero,
encadenando sus manos
que moldean la cerámica pulida
y que labran la tierra,
a la máquina de la esclavitud.

Espectro mercantil,
mordido por el ansia del poder.
Militantes de Diego Portales
putrefactos en cadáveres hombres,
mordidos por la vanidad del Culebrón,
envelecidos por el ansia del poder.

THE MURDERED DEFENCE 1

They have come to nail their exterminating banners
onto our fruitful earth.
They have come to sadden our sky
with their graveyard doors,
with their prison windows.
They have come to nail upon the earth
the law of their vile dogs,
in the boring vanity of the great male snake,
who strikes
and strangles and suppresses
the effort of the workers,
chaining their hands
which shape the shining clay,
which work the earth,
to the machinery of his enslavement.

Phantom of big business
bitten by the itch of power,
militant of the Diego Portales tendency,
rotting in the bodies of dead men,
bitten by the vanity of the great male snake
degraded by the itch of power.

Dragones fueron los que irrumpieron
nuestro espacio astronómico,
oscureciéndolo con gases tóxicos
brotando de sus fosas nasales,
cortando dementemente el cielo de nuestros ojos
con su espada aterradora del sonido atómico.
Y con sus lenguas infernales
deliraron fuego en La Moneda,
en su lenguaje de muerte expandida
y en su código secreto de cementerios clandestinos.
Allí en los campos furtivos
donde brota una rosa silvestre,
o allá en las profundidades del mar
donde nace la perla en la ostra.
Allá donde se reproducen con gran alevosía del régimen
cruces de difuntos Desaparecidos.

They were dragons who burst
into our familiar space defined by stars
darkening it with toxic gases
which flamed from their flaring nostrils,
crazily cutting the sky from our eyes
with the shattering blade of their atomic bomb.
And with hellish tongues
poured a delirium of fire over La Moneda,
in their language of death expanded
in their secret code of clandestine graveyards.
There in the field
where a wild rose sprouts furtively
or deep in the ocean
where the pearl is born in the oyster.
There, where in the regime's enormous treachery
crosses are hammered out for the dead Desaparecidos.

M.B.

2

Resiste la conciencia a las metrallas de aviones acorazados,
resistiendo con mi cuerpo solo,
con mis peñascos solo,
y con ella la tierra,
es mi mejor amada.
La lluvia, la tormenta y el mar,
el trueno, el viento y el cielo,
son mis mejores aliados.
Trueno es mi voz,
rayo es mi arma
que fulminará al Dictador.

2

Conscience resists the machine guns of ironclad fighter planes
resisting with my single body
with my crags alone
and with conscience, the earth
it is my best love.
Rain, storm and the sea
thunder, wind and the sky
are my best allies.
Thunder is my voice
I am armed with lightning
it will dazzle the dictator.

M.B.

3

Floreciente divina,
creciente peregrina,
voz ardiente
que se escucha cantada
en mujeres proletarias.
Frescas frutas de mujeres,
sus eros asesinados,
sus amores fusilados.

Araucoamericano
de tierras fulgentes
del sur austral,
más allá de un punto cardinal
poblado de geografías insurgentes.
Con su hombre desnudo
su cuerpo al aire,
la tierra fértil enamorada,
en una actitud de entrega
al padre sol que la fecunda
con sus rayos de éxtasis,
iluminando todos sus vacíos
y pasajes secretos.

Con el corazón afectuoso
de su luz productiva,
engendra a su hija
tan hermosa como la madre
y tan rebelde como el padre.
Es una hija insurrecta,
que aparece con el fuego crepusculario
cuando aparece la aurora.

3

Divine flowering,
strange wandering growth,
voice burning
in the songs
of working class women.
Women like newly ripened fruit
their murdered loves,
their slaughtered eros.

Arauco-Americano
from the glowing lands
of the deepest south,
from beyond a compass point
people with rebel geographies,
with its man, naked,
corporeal in the clean air,
its land fruitful, in love
in that posture of surrender
to the Sun-father who impregnates her
with ecstatic light,
illumining all cavernous hollows
and secret passages.

He begets his daughter
in the glowing tenderness
of his creating light,
beautiful as her mother,
rebellious as her father,
a daughter of struggle,
who emerges in the fiery dusk
and in the moment of dawn.

Es una bella amazona,
armada con un poderoso escudo
de metales amalgamados,
ofrenda de la madre,
y una gran espada de helios,
ofrenda del padre.

Viene junto a la aurora,
a liberar a todos sus habitantes,
a proteger a toda la natura,
a limpiar los cielos contaminados,
a reforestar todas las tierras
que se volvieron áridas
con el comercio de los bosques,
entonces brotará definitivamente
de la tierra fértil,
el árbol del futuro.

El viento sur arrastra consigo
su brisa de llanto diluviano,
alimento del fuego.
Y cuando acabe el fuego,
pueblo que es fuego ardiendo,
fuego que es mi brisa,
mi sangre.
Sangre que es pueblo combatiendo,
tierra adusta ardiendo en llamas.
Fuego de Marte,
fuego es el sol
que da vida a nuestra tierra,
y cuando acabe el fuego. Muero.

She is beatiful, Amazon,
armed with a heavy shield
of fused metal,
her mother's gift,
and with a great helium sword
her father's gift.

She comes next to the dawn
to liberate a whole people,
to protect an entire nature,
to clean the damaged skies,
to replant all the deforested land,
turned into desert
when their woods were sold off.
Only then,
once and for all,
the tree of the future will sprout
out of the fruitfull earth.

The south winds brings with it
its breeze of flood and tears,
it feeds the fire.
And when the fire is over,
a people who burn like fire,
a fire which is my breeze,
my blood.
Blood of a people in struggle,
harsh land burning in flames.
A fiery Mars,
fire which is the sun
giving life to our earth,
and when that fire ends I die.

M.B.

4

Resiste Resistencia
que sigue,
ojo inmenso de luna
que crece,
una nohe estrellada
te señala el camino,
en el bosque guarda
el relámpago y el rayo,
vendaval que golpea
las puertas liberadas
y el mar que borra
las ventanas carcelarias.

4

Resist Resistance
that follows
immense lunar eye
that grows,
one starry night
shows you the way
in the forest guarding
the flash and the lightning,
gale that pounds
on the liberated doors
and the sea that erases
the prison windows.

A.M.C.S.

5

Pobladas de vientre largo,
retorcido y dado vuelta.
Poblaciones callampas
equilibradas de hambre,
de masacres y enfermedades.
Sed de desierta ansiedad
que arranca la garganta
evaporando las salivas,
entonces los labios de greda
perdien la humedad
de sus besos de cristal
con palabras que se desprenden
y se vuelan, en un acto
de delirio de la historia,
que busca el equilibrio del universo,
de la justicia y las leyes,
al hombre Nuevo-Cosmológico.
Desierto rocoso, basural de congoja,
afloran de esta tierra compuesta
mis campamentos heroicos
Caupolicán, Lautaro, Arauco,
Camilo Torres, Camilo Cienfuegos,
Ché Guevara,
Campamento Luis Emilio Recabarren,
Miguel Henríquez, Salvador Allende,
Victor Jara, Pablo Neruda,
Campamento Primero de Mayo.
Vivan mis campamentos heroicos,
ellos cada uno un poema
una canción de gesta, una epopeya.

5

Peopled with a long stomach,
twisted and turned inside out,
shanty towns
balanced by hunger,
massacres and illness.
Thirst from abandoned hope
that wrenches throats
evaporating saliva,
then the clay lips
lose the moisture
of their crystal kisses
with words that come loose
and take flight, in an act
of historical delirium,
that is searching for the balance of the universe,
of the justice of laws,
for the new Cosmological Man.
Rocky desert, rubbish heap of anguish,
from this composite soil are sprouting
my heroic camps
Caupolicán, Lautaro, Arauco,
Camilo Torres, Camilo Cienfuegos,
Ché Guevara,
Luis Emilio Recabarren Camp,
Miguel Henríquez, Salvador Allende,
Victor Jara, Pablo Neruda,
May 1st Camp.
Long live my heroic camps,
each one of them a poem
a *chanson de geste*, an epic.

A.M.C.S.

36

Que resuciten las estrellas caídas
en los campos de Chile
y sus ancestros naturales.
Que renazcan con las flores libetarias
al clamor que trae el arco iris
ABAJO LA TIRANIA
Y MAS ALEGRIA.
Que despierte de la piedra
el NO IDENTIFICADO,
revelación de nuestros sentimientos al tiempo
en estruendosa denuncia milenaria.
Que los volcanes purifiquen la tierra
de la Gran Metrópolis Dióxido de Carbono.
Rómpase por fin el cristal,
las cárceles de la dictadura,
las criminales comadrejas
con sus escuadrones de la muerte.
Entonces la tierra ya no escuchará
perdón ni clemencia de sus destructores,
la promesa del día final en las manos del pueblo,
que se desborde el metal rojo liberado.

6

May the fallen stars rise
in the fields of Chile
and her natural ancestors.
May they be reborn with the libertarian flowers
to the clamour of the rainbow
DOWN WITH TYRANNY
AND MORE JOY.
May the UNIDENTIFIED MAN, WOMAN,
be roused from the stone
revelation of our sentiments to time
in vociferous millenary denouncement.
May volcanoes purify the soil
of the Great Carbon-Dioxide Metropolis.
May the glass break
the prisons of dictatorship,
the wicked weasels
with their death squadrons.
Then the earth will no longer listen
to pardon or clemency from its destroyers
the promise of the final day in the peoples' hands
let the liberated red metal overflow.

A.M.C.S.

SUEÑOS

DREAMS

SUEÑOS DEMENTES

'Sueños dementes y que sin embargo
nos parecen razonables mientras los soñamos'
Hebbel: *Diario* 1842

Rosalinda, ¿recuerdas a nuestro
compañero de viaje
José María Cristian?

Quien se gastaba el día
pensando qué sería de él
cuando muriera,
pero tuvo un presentimiento
quizás ya había muerto
y poseído por ese sentimiento
volvía a hundirse en otro sueño.

Todo le pareció una gran aventura
o una pesadilla que se iba haciendo realidad,
desde cuando se embarcó
en una nave hacia la mar.

Se fue adentrando de cuerpo entero
por entre lenguas olas
al encuentro de un deseo
que se agitaba y bramaba dentro de su vientre:
soñar, soñar, vivir para soñar.

Siempre se sintió atraído por la mar,
sumergido en el origen de la creación de la vida,
y sin embargo, le aterraba ser tragado
por su garganta insaciable.

DEMENTED DREAMS

'Demented dreams which seem reasonable
while we are dreaming them'
Hebbel, *Diary* 1842

Rosalinda, do you remember
our travelling companion,
José María Cristian?

He spent his days wondering
what would become of him
after he died,
yet had a feeling
he might be already dead
and thus overwhelmed
slumped back in another dream.

It seemed an adventure
or nightmare come true
from the time he embarked
on a ship for the sea.

Wholly surrendered
among tongues of waves,
driven to meet
the insistence inside him:
I must have my dream.

He was always drawn by the sea,
to wallow in the life source,
yet its insatiable gorge
appalled him.

Fue como el cumplimiento de una profecía,
el diálogo con los idiomas de la cultura,
medir la distancia que los años separan
y recorrer los mundos que en sus aguas distan.

Eramos los pasajeros urgentes,
los expulsados de la tierra,
los refugiados de la muerte
o los valientes sin victoria ni gloria.

¿Cómo saber entonces cual iba a ser
nuestro destino emergente?
Nadie iba a quedarse en lugar alguno.

Había que parar el mundo
o anclar nuestra nave de los sueños,
porque había que bajarse a tierra algún día,
no se podía seguir navegando a la deriva toda una vida.

Muchos dejaron sus pies caminando una nostalgia,
pasos que se hundían por calles desconocidas,
perdiéndose en la niebla soledad de un puerto triste
o nave anclada en una bahía de la angustia.

José María Cristian confesó una vez
que nunca volvería a bajar a tierra
y cuando atracabamos al Puerto Santa Fe
o Desesperanza, sea puerta de entrada o de salida,
el solía dormirse en la silla de sus sueños.

Una noche despertó por un viento insistente
que golpeaba incesante las puertas de la nave
que negaban a cerrarse.

Prophecy come to pass
to speak in the culture's tongues,
measure the space of years
and reach worlds waters divided.

We were the hard-pressed pilgrims,
exiles from our land,
refugees from death,
brave without victory or glory.

How then could we know
what our fate would be?
Nowhere would any of us ever be at home.

It would mean stopping the world
or mooring our dreamship,
having to land one day
and not drift all our life long.

Many anchored in sorrowful bays,
then trod homesick roads
down grim ports' unknown streets
and were lost in lonely fog.

Cristian once confessed
he would never land again,
and when we docked at Santa Fe
or Despair, sailing in, sailing out,
in his dreams he slept on.

One night a strong wind woke him
banging the ship's doors,
which would not shut tight.

Afuera el agua se azotaba con ira
de la lluvia del destierro
contra los cristales de la claraboya
por donde miraba José María Cristian.

Entonces se incorporó y corrió por las escaleras
que lo llevaban a salas y despachos vacíos;
todos habían desaparecido como fantasmas
sin dejar huellas de sus existencias
en aquel barco deshabitado.

Un hielo le recorrió el cuerpo con estupor
haciéndolo sentir un cadáver desnudo
al contemplar lo que las olas traían:
venían subiendo y bajando una tras otra,
arrastrando consigo la fría corriente de Humbolt,
cuerpos desnudos de hombres, mujeres y niños
de quienes fueron quizás tripulantes y pasajeros.

Sus miradas sin perfil
ancladas en el fondo de la mar,
se estrellaban con crueldad
contra el cascarón del barco
que se balanceaba de un lado para otro,
las olas fueron dejando a bordo los cuerpos desnudos.

Y llegó hasta donde sus ojos podían tocar
la gran estrella que había amado,
y que en su período de vida
siempre estuvo distante en sus noches
sin que nunca le llegara abrazar su luz.

Outside the waters roared
and rain of exile
beat against the porthole window
through which he peered.

He rose and ran upstairs
to vacant rooms and offices,
vanished ghosts all gone.
The ship was untenanted.

Ice gripped him
to a corpse stripped.
He saw what the waves bore
up and down, one after another,
on the cold Humbolt current:
naked corpses, men, women and children,
crew and passengers.

Falling faceless to the sea's floor,
buffeted against the ship's keel,
rocked from side to side
or washed up on board by waves.

He stood where his eyes now met
the great star he had loved,
who throughout her whole life
had nightly been far from him,
so he could not embrace her light.

Ella había sido una mujer hermosa
que se había apagado,
y que ahora yacía tendida,
desnuda y sin vida
a bordo de aquel barco deshabitado.

Y en un acto de reflexión gritó con desesperación:
mi vida no acaba en este sueño.
Y negándose a aceptar su soledad irreversible
la quizo resucitar dándole fuego a sus labios
y sus antorchas manos se posaron
en sus pechos ya petrificados.

Se hundió entre sus miembros dolientes
ciego por su corazón ignito
hasta quedar agonizante bajo su frío silencio.
Y la nave se fue desvaneciendo con la niebla de la mar.

She had been a beautiful woman.
Extinguished now she lay
naked and lifeless
on board the deserted ship.

He cried out in despair:
My life shall not end in this dream!
Refusing his irreversible solitude,
with the warmth of his lips
he tried to revive her
and cupped her cold breasts
with his burning hands.

He sank into her
with his blind heart on fire,
till her cold silence burst it.
The ship sailed on and was lost in mist.

D.L.

PRIMER NACIMIENTO

ORIGINS

PRIMER NACIMIENTO

Tu infancia cabalgó por los rieles del gran tren lastrero
que viajaba al corazón de la tierra de La Frontera
donde los vientos entre pinos y colihues
traen a la memoria escenas de combates terribles
entre mapuches y españoles.

Eran perdices, loicas, mirlos y torcazas
por no decir todas las aves de tu bosque natal
iban a guardar sus secretos
en los nidos de tu infancia.

También eran escarabajos, grillos y mariposas
por no decir todos los insectos y coleópteros
de tu foresta ecológica
iban a enseñarte su metamorfosis
y sus secretos mitológicos.

Iban a librar sus nacimientos en tus manos
a identificarse en tu efusión verbal
en la palabra no escrita de tu imaginación.

Pan y palabra fue la gracia generosa
que nutrió la pasión de tu infancia,
ofrenda de la tierra del primer nacimiento,
allá creciste con la nobleza del paisaje
y el vigor de su clima.

ORIGINS

Your childhood galloped along the rails of the great ballast train
which travelled into the heart of La Frontera country
where the winds among the pines and the bamboos
bring back to the memory scenes of dreadful battles
between the Mapuche and the Spanish.

There were partridges, thrushes, blackbirds and wild pigeons
not to mention all the birds of your native woods
they were going to score their secrets
in the nests of your childhood.

There were also beetles, crickets and butterflies
not to mention all the insects and coleoptera
in your ecological forest
they were going to teach you their changes
and their secret mythologies.

They were going to deliver their births in your hands
to come to know themselves shaped in your language
in the unwritten word of your imagination.

Bread and the word were the generous grace
that nourished your passionate childhood
an offering from the land of your origins.
You grew there with the nobility of the landscape
hardy like its climate.

Allá tus manos se volaron con las aves libertarias
y tus cabellos verdes
se trenzaron con el oscuro follaje
de los bosques desafiantes al sol.

Allá con alas huracanadas
de viento y lluvia
germinaron los poemas
del primer nacimiento.

Your hands flew with the birds discovering freedom.
And your green hair
was braided up with dark leaves
in woods that challenge the sun.

There with hurricane wings
with wind and rain
were seeded the poems
of your origins.

M.B.

LA VOZ DE LA MADERA

He aquí los árboles solemnes
bosques de hombres y mujeres
que se entregan por entero
a tu palabra
la voz de la madera.
He aquí donde comienza a latir
la celulosa de tus miembros
la greda que es tu carne.

Aqui laten y aquí yacen
enterrados, subterráneos y secretos
tus sueños sin fronteras,
para renacer en las alturas,
en la purificación de la atmósfera,
en el nacimiento del oxígeno,
latiendo en cada poema
árbol que crece, nace y florece.

Tu voz legendaria de los bosques
se identifica con el canto del leñador,
se cristaliza con el canto de las vertientes
y las aguas que unen la región de los lagos,
junto a la noche sin fondo
donde tu corazón noctámbulo persigue a la luna.

VOICE OF THE WOOD

Here are majestic trees,
forests of men and women
listening entranced to your word,
the voice of the wood.
Here it starts to beat,
the cellulose of your limbs,
the matter which is your flesh.

Here throb your boundless dreams,
underground secretly,
then reappear above
giving oxygen
to renew the atmosphere,
pulse through every poem,
as a tree sprouts, grows and blooms.

Your ancestral forest voice
is one with woodcutter's song,
sings too in the slopes
and waters linking lakes
in deep darkness,
where your nightwalking heart
follows the moon.

Sí, tu voz es un eco en la noche.
Sí, es el viento que canta con voz ronca pero solemne
al cruzar por el territorio de su verde espesura.
Es la voz que invita a compartir pasión y vida
a la pusilánime luna,
quien pestañea como si fuera un ojo medroso
entre los cerros y las nubes
porque no se atreve a encontrarse con su amado en su morada.

Es tu voz que persigue a la luna
en la danza de los salmones,
buscando el nacimiento de la muerte en las alturas
para ganarse las estrellas que vienen naciendo.
Asimismo corrías ansioso por la noche en vano
en un desesperado intento de poseerla para siempre.

Así lo revela tu palabra en la voz de la madera
que es un designio escrito con éxtasis y catástrofe:

'Los otros árboles ancianos
se iban tumbando
con la edad de los años.
El viento
les iba dando sepultura.'

Your voice is echoing night,
windroar hoarse but solemn
crossing the land's thick green.
To passion and life
it invites the timid moon,
as she peeps out shyly
between hills and clouds,
for she daren't meet her lover at home.

Your voice follows the moon
in the salmon's dance
to spawn and perish upriver,
approach the emerging stars.
Through blackness you too rush desperately
wanting to possess her forever.

Your word is revealed
in the voice of the wood,
pattern written
in ecstasy and catastrophe:

'The other ancient trees fall
as the years pass.
The wind gives them burial.'

D.L.

LA TIERRA HA DE QUEDAR LIBRE PARA SIEMPRE

Un grano que colapsó de aquella ventana verde
penetró por tus poros fértiles y echó raices.

Creció entre sonidos de campanas
y los bosques balsámicos de la región.
Se alimentó de todas las hojas minerales del subsuelo
y fue subiendo hasta juntarse con la gran noche
que cimbra las sombras con vientos estupefactos.

Atuendos indígenas encarnaron
imágenes inmaculadas de la tierra,
fueron a prenderse junto a las estrellas encendidas
para brillar en tu copa de la noche.

Campana verde que sostienen los robles hiperbólicos
pinos insignes y araucarias.

Los árboles se levantaron junto a los Mapuches
con un estandarte de liberación nacional
baluarte de los aguerridos mocetones.

Allá, conquistadores de la colonización
y de la explotación
se los tragó la tierra para siempre,
se los tragaron los bosques por sus raices
porque la tierra ha de quedar libre para siempre.

THE EARTH MUST STAY FREE FOREVER

A seed which dropped from that green dome
pierced your fertile pores and put down roots.

It germinated among bell sounds
and the region's balmy woods.
It fed on all the subsoil's leafmould minerals
and grew up till it reached the great dark,
which swayed the shadows with drowsy winds.

Immaculate pictures of earth
embodied in native dress
went to be pinned up with the stars
to shine in your bowl of night.

Green bell sustaining hyperbolical oaks,
monkey puzzles and noble pines.

The trees rose with the Mapuches,
to a flag of national freedom,
stronghold of warrior braves.

There colonising exploiting conquistadors
were swallowed by earth forever.
Trees swallowed them through their roots
because the earth must stay free forever.

D.L.

EPITAFIOS FORESTALES

Tus manos van naciendo en la madera
y con ella árboles y manos van creciendo,
consagrando canto y reforestación
en la rotación del sol y de la luna,
en su juramento de sangre y fuego con la tierra.

Tus designios escritos con mitológica mano
saben a resinas de araucarias,
robles, insignes y eucaliptos,
olmos, castaños y avellanos
que van seduciéndose a la vida.

Van a cobrar vida
en la transformación
de la olorosa tabla roja,
que va construyendo
la casa ecológica del pueblo.

FOREST EPITAPHS

Yours hands are born in wood,
thus grow hands and trees
in sacred song and reafforestation,
turning of sun and moon
covenant sealed in fire and blood.

Your mythological plans
taste of resin and monkey puzzle,
noble oak and eucalyptus,
elm, chestnut and hazel,
sweetly luring to life.

And they live on
in the transformation
of scented red timber,
which is building
the people's ecological dwelling.

D.L.

VEN SEAMOS

SO LET'S LIVE

VEN SEAMOS

Vagabundear me aburre por estas calles amarillas,
también pisar la ausencia de esta playa desolada;
te invito a que seamos, ven seamos.
A descolgar la soledad y el abandono
de fósiles fríos y cuerpos sobresalientes.
¿Por qué no subimos la escalera caracol
con el tenaz deseo de suspendernos en la esfera del reloj?
Vaciar los números por el espiral
cayendo así cual grito en el eco: seamos, ven seamos.

Pero un tiro causó conmoción en el espacio
y un revoloteo repentino de gaviotas
quedó estancado en la noche.
El aire se llenó de luces feroces
que rastreaban huellas en el vacío.
Irrumpieron sombras con ladridos de caza
acallar estas palabras en una voz herida en el cerco.
¿Fue que nuestras ansias despertaron sospechas allá abajo?

Nuestra respiración que pendía de un hilo de saliva
al vaivén de otros astros
se cortó al zumbido iracundo de los sables.
¡Silencio! !Ocúltate! !Véte!
Me gritaba, te gritaba.
¡Muere en la rueda! Gritaban.
¡Ata tu lengua a las varas de una carreta y muere!
Me gritaban, gritaban.
Así tu secreto y el mío se secaron entre nuestras rodillas
y nuestros cuerpos parecieron a otros cuerpos
que se esparcían bajo la luz morada
en un paisaje de naturaleza muerta.

SO LET'S LIVE

I'm sick of roaming through these yellow streets
and pacing the absence of this desolate shore;
I invite you: let's live, so let's live.
To heal the lonely abandon
of cold fossils, misshapen bodies,
why don't we climb the winding stair,
up and up to hang on the clock dial?
Empty the numbers down the spiral
to fall like a cry into echo:
Let's live, so let's live.

But a shot caused commotion in space
and a sudden flutter of seagulls
stopped in the night.
Ferocious lights filled the air,
searching for tracks in the void.
Shadows broke in, hounds in full cry
hunting these words, surrounding this voice.
Were we then suspect because of our longing?

Our breath which hung on a thread of saliva
among the to-ing and fro-ing of other stars
was cut short by the swish of sabres.
Silence! Hide! Be gone!
Shouted at me. Shouted at you.
Die on the wheel! They shouted.
Harness your tongue to the cart shafts and die!
They shouted at me. They shouted.
Thus your secret and mine ran dry between our knees.
And our bodies looked like other bodies
strewn under purple light
in a still-life landscape.

Chorro de luz caliente viajando en profundidad de huesos
en un vuelo albo de melancolía
para vivir allí dentro blanco entero.
Así avanzabamos a ciegas entre las sombras
buscando los ojos
la estrella presente
y la rosa viva.

Y si la ida y el regreso
son dos sueños que no acaban
y siguen su viaje sin nosotros,
¿para qué persignarnos con viejas mandas
a sabiendas que no hay tal ciencia cierta?

Que fuimos destartalados ramilletes de elocuencia,
un desparramo de pensamientos en lenguaje casto
y que servimos de testigos a tantas mentiras y verdades,
de historias que navegan por la mente
como iluso viajero que entra y sale
por una puerta incierta del tiempo,
la puerta que cierra los arcos de triunfo
y da a un salón blanquísimo sin hora alguna.

Allí esperé sin día ni noche
el retorno de tus pasos.
Busqué en vano tu cuerpo entre figurillas de hielo
y la estatua que esperaba perdió su forma,
simplemente todos los días se deshojaron iguales,
racimo desgajándose en lluvia monotonía.

Rush of warm light deep through the bones
in a white flight of melancholy,
absolute whiteness.
Blindly we groped among shadows
seeking eyes,
the shining star
and the living rose.

And if the leaving and the return
are two dreams which go on and on,
and they continue their journey without us,
why cross ourselves with ancient commandments
when we know there is no such certainty?

We were shabby ragbags of eloquence,
a squander of thoughts in nice language
and we witnessed so many lies and truths,
stories that sail through our minds
dream-travelling in and out
of an uncertain time door,
door which closes triumphal arches
and opens into a drawing room,
whiter than white, where there is no time.

There dayless and nightless I listened
for your reapproaching footsteps.
I looked for your body in vain
among standing ice figures
but the statue I wanted lost its shape,
day followed day like falling leaves,
grapes drop from the bunch like dreary rain.

Pasos retrospectivos
entrando de espaldas por el espejo quebrado,
bajar las mismas escaleras subidas
o tal vez estos mismos versos en su regreso
sean una carta con otro manifiesto.

Y bajo una cerrada bruma púrpura
uno tras otro iban cruzando por el gran salón
blanquísimo del Castillo Visconte:
imágenes descoloridas de los amigos idos,
mi madre cantando y comiendo uvas,
el perfil de las sombras de los hermanos Pablo,
Marx, Lenin y la Mona Lisa,
caretas guerreras de los Mayas,
el caballo de Guernica en agonía trepando una muralla
y las luces feroces cortaban la noche.

Afuera, de pronto una présaga quietud
se apodera del paisaje,
la irrumpe una bandada de pájaros en vuelo despavorido
que en instantes parecieron
que se hubiesen pegado en la atmósfera.

Detrás se siente el agitado terremoto
y todo cuerpo viviente sufre.
Movimiento desarticulado de la tierra.
Una estampida de voraces dinosauros.
Gruñe un perro y el aire vibra entrecortado.
Todos huyen y desaparecen en cualquier dirección
y las campanas suenan por su cuenta.

En ese momento sentí frío en mi memoria
bajo la sombra de un árbol que quiso y no fue.

Backward through the broken mirror,
down the stairs they'd been up,
or perhaps these very lines coming home
are a letter with a different message.

Under thick purple fog
one after another they passed
through the great, whiter than white
drawing room of Castle Visconte.
Discoloured images of absent friends,
my mother singing and eating grapes,
silhouette of the Pablo brothers,
Marx, Lenin and Mona Lisa,
warlike masks of the Mayas,
the Guernica horse in its agony climbing the wall
and ferocious lights cutting the night.

Outside an ominous silence
suddenly possesses the land,
broken by a flock of birds in panic flight,
which quickly look stuck to the sky.

Behind them the earthquake shudders,
every living creature suffers
and the earth writhes.
Stampede of hungry dinosaurs.
A dog growls and the air vibrates.
All flee in every direction
and the bells clang.

At that moment I felt cold in my memory
under the shade of a tree
which wanted to be and was not.

Desde entonces que navego
dentro de tus ojos entristecidos,
en el puerto de tu sonrisa con mi boca ciega,
entre las aguas del zodíaco
y las islas de tus senos.

Idoneidad revolucionaria que resiste caer fusilada
bajo la utopía de círculos cerrados.
Somos el beso que corre con la serpiente
sobre la cálida arena.
Quisiéramos ser mariposa liberada de su capullo,
la primavera triunfante con pétalos y guirnaldas,
bailar el vals de los amores en el carnaval El Sol.

Since then I sail in your sad eyes
and your smile's haven with my blind mouth,
between zodiac waters
and the isles of your breasts.

Revolutionary power
which resists being shot down,
under the utopia of closed circles.
We are the kiss that runs with the serpent
on the warm sand.
We want to be butterfly chyrsalis-freed,
triumphant spring with blossoms and garlands,
dance the love waltz in the El Sol carnival.

D.L.

STONEHENGE

Neblina hunde el horizonte
y sobre piedras gravita el firmamento,
viento que no pisa su umbral,
de cerca siento su silencio.

Si regresara el bumerang
por estas ventanas de círculo glacial,
con cordura deslumbraría lengua perdida
en el centro de la esfera,
eslabón locuaz de las estrellas.

Tacto de milenios resbalan por el índice,
panteón que fija punto cruz de los opuesto,
mide la luz más larga del estío,
como blanca noche interminable del invierno.

De ese mismo horizontal
cuelga incógnita la luna,
tal sol cruzando las fronteras
y la muerte en el ángulo perfecto.

STONEHENGE

Fog envelopes the horizon,
firmament gravitates on stones,
wind does not pass their threshold,
I feel how still they are.

If the boomerang returned
through these gaps in the glacial circle,
it would strike a lost tongue true,
there at the sphere's centre,
where stars meet and converse.

Millenial forefinger indicates
a pantheon of intersecting opposites,
measuring summer's long days
as white winter endless night.

From this same horizontal
hangs the moon unknown
as the sun crossing frontiers
and death at a perfect angle.

D.L.

ESCOPETISTAS

HUNTERS

ESCOPETISTAS DE LA AURORA

Sentado en la piedra que marca tu ausencia
me sumo a la noche mantener en pie el firmamento,
punto de confesión equidistante
en que gira el carrusel de los dioses.
Entonces hablan las piedras
en su lenguaje por sí solas
y flores escarchadas de puños oprimidos
se zafan monótona cuerda del tiempo.
Tus duros besos de luna querida amiga
se colgaron de la mirada con silencio de estrellas,
calma desnuda de ardiente impaciencia
en copa de ojos invertida hacia dentro,
visión a toda cercanía que por fin despierta.

¡Levántate Auristela!
en un grito de unísona conciencia.
Levántate con tu verdad rompetinieblas,
alborada encantada de locura o libertad,
rayo rompehielos del corazón que traza
la linea del horizonte con cromos de ilusión
en dramáticas piruetas de golondrinas
que se estrellan con el paisaje.

Tronan los cuernos con pólvora y ladridos
afín al recuerdo, se aparece el Duque,
el ángel de la luz tras su heráldica,
el venado de los Andes su mal de rosas.

DAWN HUNTERS

I sit on the stone recording your absence
and help night hold up the firmament
fixed point from which to contemplate
the merry-go-round of the gods.
Then the stones speak
in their own stone language
and oppressed fists which are frost flowers
undo time's ancient knot.
Dear friend your hard moon kisses
hung about with silent stars
are the calm of burning impatience,
eyes turned inwards
upon an intimate vision awaking.

Arise Auristela!
Come to yourself and shout.
Arise with your truth
that shatters darkness,
to madness or freedom's dawn,
your ice-breaking heart-ray
tracing hope's rosy horizon
in dazzling swallow whirls.

Sound of horns with shots and barking
until in memory the Duke appears,
angel of light hunting his heraldic trophy,
the Andean stag sick for roses.

Las indias se bañaban
en la turquesa repleta de flores
en el jardín del oráculo.
El faisán, un cronómetro fiel, gritaba
su ruin desesperanza al mediodía, augurio
para quien perdió el rostro en el bosque
y el Huemúl delante comiéndole las rosas.

La escopeta en alto
el ojo en la mira
y el venado pastando.

Una pirámide de conciencia se levanta,
memoria que se precipita por las canaletas de la noche,
las emociones que rodan por la telescópica del Duque
y sangre de plata plenilunia.
Por cada laberinto que cruza con la mira
un coro de oraciones en lamentos,
una ópera de rock húngaro con bocinazos estridentes
y sonidos de vidrios quebrados.

En un reflejo de lentes hacia adentro
en vértigos de medianoche
se ve el rostro descubierto,
el pie que patina
en la pradera del otro,
la bota lustrada que delata
hedor a mierda pura.

The Indian women bathed
in the flower-strewn turquoise
in the oracle garden.
The pheasant, faithful timekeeper, screeched
its despair at noon, portent
for him who lost his face in the forest
and the *Huemúl* standing there eating his roses.

Gun cocked
eye on its sight
and the stag grazing.

A thought pyramid rises,
a memory hurtles along night's gutters,
feelings rush down the Duke's telescopic sight
and the silver full moon shows blood.
Chorus of prayers and laments
weaving through labyrinths,
Hungarian rock opera strident with horns
and crash of breaking glass.

In the inward-reflecting lenses
of midnight dizziness
he discovers his face –
his foot skates over
another's meadow,
the polished boot
smelling of pure shit.

¿Ya presa del fastidio,
qué le importaba
que gritara un buho,
que llorara una guagua
o que matara a un venado?

Ante los ojos del Huemúl
todo espacio abierto es venerado,
cautiva mirada de Ocho Venados,
noble cacique mixteca,
guerrero de mil pueblos,
y compañero de cinco princesas.
Musas enmudecidas
por los horrores de la conquista,
gobiernos medusas
infestadas de dictaduras
solo el mirlo blanco comunica
en la cresta del venado.

Pero una vez bajo la cruz
los dados ocultos bajo el tacón
sueltan brutalmente los segundos
ay, vida que corre por laberintos de pares y nones,
ay, índice que resbala hasta el fondo de la argolla
y el gatillo que detona su fatal polución.

Un tridente obsidiano atravesó la memoria
el último año 52 de un centenario,
a los pies una rosa a medio morder
y el Huemúl tumbado cual árbol caído.
De sus temples una mariposa con las alas sangrando,
cual capa que cae sobre los hombros
le abraza el alma con escalofríos.

Already he feels
what does it matter
that an owl should hoot,
a baby cry,
or a stag be shot?

In the eyes of the *Huemúl*
every open space is holy,
captive gaze of *Ocho Venados*,
the noble Mixtec chief
warrior of a thousand tribes
and lover of five princesses.
Muses struck dumb
by the horrors of conquest.
Medusa governments
dictator-infested.
Only the white thrush speaks
from the stag's antlers.

But once under the cross
the hidden dice under the heel
brutally gamble away the seconds,
life runs through mazes of odds and evens,
finger slides into position
and the trigger releases its fatal pollution.

Memory recalls a flint trident,
Aztec centenary year 52.
At his feet a half bitten rose
and the *Huemúl* lies like a fallen tree.
From his forehead a butterfly with bleeding wings
drops like a cloak on the Duke's shoulders,
envelopes his shuddering soul.

Triunfante el Duque consternado,
su honor se descolora en los rosales,
su metamorfosis en alacrán,
otro escorpión le devora el interior
dejándole vacía su caparazón.

La escopeta en alto
el ojo en la mira
y el venado pastando.

The triumphant Duke dismayed,
his honour fades among the roses
his scorpion metamorphosis,
another scorpion devours his innards
leaving his empty shell.

Gun cocked
eye on its sight
and the stag grazing.

D.L.

Auristela is a Spanish Christian name which means 'Dawn path'.
Huemúl is the Andean stag. It inhabits the south of Chile.
Guagua is the Quechua word for baby.
Ocho Venados was the name of great Aztec warrior, 'Eight Stags'.

FLOR DE LOTO

Yo que vi mi juventud en mi casa
medrar en tul de amapolas blancas y negras.
En mis manos maduraban las ciruelas
al escuchar las ansias de la mar
poseída en un azul profundo de estrellas,
junto a la playa de cenizas del volcán Llaimá,
flor de loto entre espejos oscuros
al fondo de un acuario de cristal.

En otro cielo caleidoscópico me dan vértigos las nubes,
verlas cruzar la cordillera a toda prisa,
horas ausentes que no acabaron mis días;
vértigos me dan el calendario y el reloj,
tal lava de volcán petrifica las manos en el surco,
como hortalizas de piedra
en un páramo de árboles sin leña.

Nave multifacética arrastrada por un viento sin estaciones,
navega entre telas blancas de blancos hongos del éxodo;
corazón que se nos vuela por la boca
para escapar y gritar por ella,
labios que besan desolación,
no así el secreto de las mieles
como tantas flores ocultas tras la semilla.

Sala de nunca acabar en su interior,
imágenes de mártires revelan la sangre escondida
tras las murallas de sal.
Se quiebra el dominio de las espadas,
la cordillera se remece al redoble de un kurtrun,
paso de guerra de los Mapuches;
voces rezan gritos de dolor de los caídos
al zumbar de los sables

LOTUS FLOWER

My childhood at home
grew in a tangle of black and white poppies.
In my hands ripened the plums
as I listened to the restless sea,
star blue to its depth.
On the ashy shore by the Llaima volcano
bloomed the lotus flower among dark mirrors
on a glass aquarium floor.

In another kaleidoscope sky,
clouds hurtling over the mountain tops
giddy the lonely hours of my never ending day;
calendar and clock are also vertigo,
as lava petrifies hands in the furrow,
stone vegetables in a waste of blasted trees.

A multifaceted ship in continual wind
sails through sheets of white exodus fungi.
My heart flies out of my mouth
to escape with a scream,
my lips kiss desolation,
this is not the honey secret
of all those flowers the seed contained.

A room goes on and on,
its martyr portraits are fresh with blood
oozing through walls of salt.
The rule of the sword is broken,
the mountains rock to a *kurtrun* rumble,
war tread of the Mapuches;
voices beseech with the pain of the fallen
as the sabres clash.

Zarzuelas y comparsas bajan a la plaza
y la tela roja flamea entre los cuernos de un toro
que brama a la muerte.
Irrumpen en la sala bandadas de gaviotas
en sinfonía de mar.
Luna es la novia descendiendo por mis sueños,
con velos y luz antártica abriga mi desnudez
y una ronda de niños cantan a nuestro alrededor.

The operetta and bands enter the square
and the red rag ripples between the bull's horns,
who roars at death.
A sea symphony of gulls bursts into the room.
The moon is the bride descending my dreams,
she veils my nakedness in antarctic light
and a ring of children sing round us.

D.L.

WEKUFES

WEKUFES

EXEQUIAS

Con un vuelo invisible de lechuza
resuena el trompe en las colinas,
así tal memoria atrapada en un eco
entierra los ojos de la machi.
Mutación que reverbera por tus poros
con los espíritus derretidos
entonces el mago bajo la fiebre de Febo
te arranca con el tacto un sonido de cristal.
Te besa en un hechizo, derritiéndote,
va llenando las copas de tí
y tu mirada se va haciendo aurora.

EXEQUIES

With the invisible flight of an owl
resounds the harp in the hills,
thus such a memory trapped in an echo
buries the eyes of the sorceress.
Mutation reverberating through your pores
with melted spirits
then magician with Phoebus' fever
plucks a crystal sound from you with his touch.
He kisses you under a spell, melting you,
pouring you slowly into the glasses
and your gaze slowly becomes dawn.

A.M.C.S.

MILLARAI

De acuerdo a la dialéctica de la mano,
a la del calidoscopio del mago,
te veo Millarai recién nacida.
Frágil copa de escarcha
que el amante deshace,
liberación del espíritu
que trepa la noche
multiplicándola de estrellas.

Dulce Aimé, Millarai,
huaca de espesuras,
carita de copihue,
encanto del conhuipa.
Millarai trompe de ausencias,
canto de huracán,
rumor de puihua negra.

Rayos de sol por los vítreos
de una catedral,
tu corazón de paisaje
floresta mapuche.
Vestida de islas
atadas a la cintura,
Millarai alcanza su estatura.

MILLARAI

By sleight of hand
and magical kaleidoscope,
I see you Millarai new born.
Delicate frost goblet
a lover melted,
your free spirit
climbs the night,
and scatters stars.

Sweet Aimé, Millarai,
huaca of thickets
copihue lily face ,
enchantment of wooded *conhuipa*.
Mapuche harp of absence,
hurricane song,
roar of the black wind, *puihua*.

Through cathedral windows,
sun's rays
are your heart's country,
Mapuche grove.
Skirted with islands
girded to her waist,
Millarai attains her stature.

En otro páramo, el reflejo
de un triángulo interior,
la versión oculta en la memoria,
te veo sacrifacada por la iglesia y el gobierno,
deforestada por el afán de plusvalía
y la turquesa de tus ojos
extirpada por la televisión.

Te veo en una penitencia de terror,
tus senos los pechos cortados de Olalla,
la cabeza de Juan el Bautista
en bandeja de plata,
la paloma degollada
de los sindicalistas de Chile.

En la recapitulación de un interrogatorio,
veo al oficial criollo
que te interroga en lengua huinca,
estadio repleto con ecos de carcajadas
tras los acordes furiosos del piano:

¿Dáme un precio Millarai?,
¿el precio de tu belleza,
del placer y de tu amor?
¿Dáme un precio por tu arte
tu ideal, tu concepción?
¿Dáme un precio Millarai?

In another reflection
inside memory's pyramid
I see you sacrificed by church and government,
disafforested by lust for profit
with television extinguishing
the turquoise of your eyes.

I see you under penance of terror
your breasts cut off like Ollala's,
your head like John the Baptist's
served on a silver plate,
as Chile's trade-unionists
are a dove with its throat cut.

In a repeated interrogation
I see the creole official
grilling you in a foreign language,
with guffaws echoing round the stadium
to furious piano chords.

Tell me how much Millarai?
What price your beauty,
pleasure and love?
How much for your art,
ideas, imagination?
Tell me how much Millarai?

Veo tu sangre que corre por la cruz,
en tu cuerpo los azotes del encomendador,
los picotazos del águila y las heridas del Ché,
¡púlsalas Tomás!,
y verás que llegan al fondo de los ojos.

En la punta de las colinas,
un campo de concentración
con prisioneros en la pica del conquistador,
mientras el orfeón de sexo y fuego
entona el himno nacional.
En otras cercanías, las princesas
con sus trenzas ardiendo
escapan de la soldadesca por los potreros
hasta que se agoniza
en círculos de sangre y mierda.

Detrás queda la tierra talada,
tristes escombros de un genocidio fascista:
una sierra desdentada con inscripciones japonesas,
un neumático americano a medio quemar,
un esqueleto suspendido en una grúa quebrada,
la armadura de un vehículo sin placa
hirviendo de culebras
y una bota militar como guarida de alacranes.

Frágil copa de nieve
que el tiempo deshace, Millarai.
Se siente que llegan, retumban
los tambores de los muertos,
torres subterráneas del cielo mapuche.

I see your blood flow down the cross
lackeys lash your body
eagles peck at it,
it bears Che's wounds.
Press them, Thomas!
You'll find they reach deep into the eyes.

In the hilltop concentration camp
prisoners speared by the conquistador
and a band bellowing sex and fire
strikes up the national hymn.
Not far away, the princesses
with burning plaits
flee the military across meadows
until death catches up and closes
a circle of blood and shit.

The ravaged country lies -
fascist genocide left it desolate -
a toothless saw with Japanese inscriptions
an American tyre half burnt.
From a broken crane hangs a skeleton,
an armoured car without number plates
seethes with vipers
and a military jackboot is a scorpion's nest.

Your are a frail snow cup
time melted, Millarai.
Now we hear them coming
and the dead drums rolling,
underground Mapuche towers.

Ahora usted mire con la paloma en el ojo,
el devenir de la puihua blanca.
Entre nubes, Millarai,
tus labios cuelgan suspendidos
sin más rostro que el cielo.

Allende su caballo de invierno
galopa por el rostro de Lautaro.
Arriba, los labios sonríen,
gesticulan, el huinca no entiende.
Nos habla, nos besa y nos traga.
Una luna anaranjada por el horizonte
desvanece silenciosamente
la agria nieve del pasado.

Now see the dove come into view
borne on the kind white wind.
Millarai among clouds,
your lips hang there,
your face is sky.

Far off her winter horse
gallops over Lautaro's face.
Up above the lips smile with a meaning
the foreigner does not understand.
They speak to us, kiss, swallow.
Over the horizon silently
a waning orange moon
now melts the past's embittered snow.

D.L.

Millarai, 'Woman of the forest' in the Mapuche language.
Aimé was a virtuous Mapuche singer.
Huaca: a Quechua god.
Conhuipa: 'mountain path'.
Copihue is a flower which grows wild in the cold humid climate of the south Chile. Its large bell-shaped petals hold a lot of water.
Trompe is the Mapuche harp, similar to the Jew's harp.
Puihua negra is a black wind, carrying volcanic ashes. It is a natural phenomenon in the Chilean Lake District.
Huinca means foreigner in Maputhungun (the Mapuche language). Here it refers to the Chileans.
Puihua blanca is a wind of white volcanic ashes in the Chilean Lake District.
Lautaro was a young Mapuche warrior during the years of the Conquest by the Spaniards in the sixteenth century.

ANNUNCIATION

ANNUNCIATION

LOS MOLINOS DE DON QUIJOTE

Por entre laberintos de avisos luminosos
cadavéricamente galopa el caballero de la Mancha,
ornamento de sus armas, una máscara de gases
y enmohecida armadura sobre el cuerpo
que a duras penas resiste Rocinante.
En cada ciudad enfrenta a monstruosos bloques de cemento,
habla de paz a los lobos en una base coheteril,
discute con gigantes hélices pegadas al suelo contaminado
cual calavera de vaca sobre una estaca en el desierto.
Vuelan hojas de un periódico en desuso por las calles sucias
como retobos de existencias arrastradas por el viento
y en un esfuerzo sublime de concentración
quisiese parar el tiro que rompe la barrera del sonido
en loca carrera con el tiempo.
Chimeneas cual cañones disparan inmundicias hacia el cielo,
finalmente, todo baja por la garganta
y se pudre la manzana en su trayecto antes de tocar el suelo.
Fuente de lluvia ácida donde agonizan las palomas,
muerte amarilla en la imaginación ancestral, desolación,
tal desmembración de los últimos matices.
Maltrecho Don Quijote pasa sin tristeza ni dolor,
la hiel del nunca arrepentido, solo enfado,
su cruzada no acaba en este páramo.
Dulcinea su destino en un reino de pinos espaciales,
brazos foliáceos que buscan
el equilibrio de las estaciones del año,
la bebida y comida autóctona, cantos.
Aún se lee en su estropeado emblema:
"Creo en la metamorfosis orgánica de la tierra"
y una brisa radioactiva diluye su silueta en otros horizontes.

DON QUIXOTE'S WINDMILLS

Between labyrinths of luminous advertisements
gallops the cadaverous knight of La Mancha,
a gas mask's the crest of his heraldic insignia
and his armour rusts to his body,
painfully carried by patient Rocinante.
In every town he encounters concrete monstrosities,
he speaks of peace to wolves at a rocket base,
argues with giant propellers jammed in polluted earth –
cattle skulls in the desert impaled.
Dead newspapers flap in the dirty streets,
packaging for lives blown on the wind
and a supreme effort of concentration
races with time to inhibit
the shot's supersonic boom.
Cannon-like chimneys disgorge their filth,
in the end it all goes down the throat
and the apple rots before reaching the ground.
Doves are poisoned by acid rain,
ancestral imagination's yellow death, desolation,
ultimate colours falling apart.
Battered Don Quixote goes on without sadness or pain,
in the gall of never repenting, only raging,
his crusade does not finish on this bleak moor.
He is going to Dulcinea in a kingdom of airy pines,
leafy arms balancing the year's seasons,
to his native food and drink, his songs.
Still his tattered emblem reads:
'I believe in the earth's organic metamorphosis.'
A radioactive breeze blurs his outline on others horizons.

D.L.

PIEDRA DE NARANJA

Palestina de velos anaranjados
como el propio dolor nuestro
oculto entre abanicos.
Ella se come su naranja
porque tiene pulpa de mártires.
Es posible que sea judía o árabe,
mujer del holocausto
de mirada desnuda,
pero nunca israelita. Nunca.
Sus lágrimas fertilizan el desierto
ya que todo secan los centuriones con sus tanques,
y ellos indiferentes
venden la naranja en el mercado.

Hoy estas cercas de púas son cruces de David
y ella coronada de espinas carga la cruz.
Reina el toque de queda
bajo un cielo cerrado de fuego.
Gaza y Cisjordania son un calvario,
fuera del alcance de toda mano,
y sin dejar un espacio de silencio,
incesante se descarga la metralla
tal oración de los nuevos colonos
que dándose cabezazos de mentira
oran y oran a la muralla de occidente.
Qué tedioso su rosario de los territorios de siempre
que escapan más alla de la linea del horizonte
hasta donde la vista agote la luz.

STONE ORANGE

Palestine of the orange veils
like our own pain
hiding behind a fan.
She eats her own orange
whose flesh is her martyrs'.
She might be Jew or Arab,
holocoust woman unveiled
but never Israeli. Never.
Her tears water the desert
that centurions' tanks have dried
and they don't care:
they take the orange to market
and sell it.

Today these barbed wire fences are crosses of David.
Crowned with thorns she carries the cross.
Curfew reigns and a gunfire curtain
is drawn over the sky.
Gaza and Transjordan are calvary,
beyond all reach,
with no space for silence.
Incessant machine guns rattle
like the new settlers' prayers
butting and butting wrong heads
at the western wall.
How tedious their eternal rosary
of territories over the horizon
stretching beyond sight and light.

Entonces uno se pregunta,
¿qué sentencia dijo Jeremías
para que la Palestina pague esta desgracia?,
¿o qué otra mierda dijo Aristóteles
para que se llegara a la exterminación de los judíos?
Yo no sé de equivalencias
pero se siente en la Palestina,
aplastada bajo la bota israelita
que penan los nazis;
y uno ve en estos jóvenes soldados,
extraterrestres que invaden el planeta.

Acabaron con un oasis,
trescientas aldeas palestinas
sepultadas bajo la arena,
pero el pueblo desentierra a sus muertos,
un ventarrón de conciencia que nos levanta la mirada
y sube como un torbellino de ánimas vivas,
mártires que reviven,
torbellino del pueblo con piedra de mártires
y nuevamente comienza a contarse la historia:
en este Ramadán llueven piedras,
porque piedra es el dolor y la ira del pueblo;
a la soldadesca zionista le llueven piedras.

Y Jalil el Wazir es un acantilado de piedras,
vuela como un cometa arrojado por una adolescente.
El Ramadán en su tercera noche,
Mahoma monta los cielos de Jerusalén
en el Pegaso de Abu Yihad,
de su galope florecen auroras en el desierto
y anuncios con campanadas de triunfo.

And we wonder
what judgment did Jeremiah pass
for Palestine to suffer so?
What other rubbish of Aristotle's
led to the Jews' extermination?
I don't know about that
but I know that in Palestine
you feel flattened under Israeli boots,
punishing nazis;
and these young soldiers
look like extraterrestrials
invading the planet.

They destroyed an oasis,
three hundred Palestinian villages
buried in sand
but the people unbury their dead,
conscience awakes in a gale
that turns to a whirlwind of living souls,
rising martyrs,
the martyrs are pebbles
on the storm wind, the people.
And history begins again:
this Ramadan rains stones,
stones are the people's anger and pain,
on the Zionist soldiery stones rain.

And Khalil al-Wazir is a bank of stones,
he flies like a comet hurled by a girl.
It is the third night of Ramadan,
Mahomed climbs the Jerusalem sky
on Abu Jihad Pegasus,
dawn galloping over the desert
and victory bells. *D.L.*

EL SILENCIO DEL ERICH FRIED

Hacia el mundo dan tus ventanales
del interior se ven los traseúntes
levantó el vuelo tu mente por la noche
cual lechuza en busca de la luna,
y de esas altas paredes de libros
nuevos espacios libres vas creando.
Es tu voz profunda y continua,
de socialismo humanista
que comunica a los delfines
en los jóvenes huérfanos del holocausto.
Es el amor que no tiene campo definido,
'es lo que es' todo y nada:
tu sonrisa en busca de realización.

Se anticipó tu hijo
en busca de una respuesta,
te traía un bombillo malo,
la lámpara del escritorio no alumbraba,
'ya lo vi padre está quemado'.
Tu te lo llevaste como quien anida
un pájaro herido entre las manos,
reparando la luz tenue
a ese cielo profundo y oscuro.

THE SILENCE OF ERICH FRIED

Your windows give onto the world,
look out to passersby,
where at night your mind flew up
like an owl seeking the moon
and from those high book walls
you keep creating liberated zones.
Insistent and deep,
your socialist humanist voice
speaks to dolphins,
young holocaust orphans.
Unfenced is this love's field,
'it is what is',
everything and nothing:
your smile wanting to get things done.

Your son said it.
Expecting you to sort it out
he brought you a dead bulb:
the desk lamp didn't work.
'I knew it was gone dad.'
You took it as if your hands
were nestling a wounded bird
and gave its little light
back to the sky and the dark.

A un acto a Neruda te invitaba,
tú me hablabas de él
de un día en Alemania.
Condenamos a la Colonia alemana
Dignidad de la dictadura
por servirle como centro de tortura,
y al podrido Franz-Joseph Strauss
un admirador de Pinochet
que acababa de morirse.
A la hora de la cena, el Rioja
llenó las copas de saludos,
brindamos por el silencio de Chile
que no durará eternamente,
el pueblo en su grito de victoria
en un son de espera en tu poema,
y unido a tu familia brindé por tí.

En el acto de esa noche,
nosotros en Londres
y tú en Alemania,
leímos a unísono
tus últimos poemas a Chile.

Y en una calle cualquiera del mundo,
un disco del tránsito te señaló
el final de una vía irreversible.
Calle de fechas coincidentes,
Neruda distó apenas de un día
a tu llegada,
a ese final que nadie llega tarde.

I invited you to a reading for Neruda.
You talked about him,
about a day in Germany.
We condemned the German Colony –
'Dignity' for the dictatorship –
used for torture.
We condemned Franz Joseph Strauss
Pinochet's rotten admirer
whose death was in the news.
At supper Rioja filled our glasses
and we drank to the silence of Chile,
which will not last forever,
to the people's hope
shouting victory in your poem,
and together with your family
I drank to you.

At the reading that night
we in London
and you in Germany
read jointly
your last poems to Chile.

And somewhere in the world
a street sign signalled
your journey's end.
Coincidence street:
Neruda's date was hardly a day away
from your arrival
there where no one can come late.

Embriagado en un soliloquio,
en vano te busqué
con las copas en candela.
Transcurso en que todos
regresan al elemento de todo,
la vuelta al tiempo elemental del suelo.
Tu retornaste a la primera
y a la única tierra,
al primer hombre, al primer río,
al primer árbol.

Tus llaves van por un torrente de luz,
para quien quiera abrir
puertas de liberación,
amplios ventanales, tu corazón,
alta columna de puños
que sostienen el cielo.

Subiste al silencioso lecho de la noche,
con cristales de estrellas en los cabellos,
como un santo contemporáneo, un revolucionario.
Te vi por última vez,
como un planeta vital,
lleno de ideas, lúcido de vida
que girabas a mi alrededor.

In a lonely drunken monologue
I addressed you in vain
keeping candle lit vigil.
Over that crossing we all
return to the universal element,
the soil's elemental time.
You were restored to the first
and only earth, first human,
first river, first tree.

You unlock a torrent of light
for all who want
to open doors of freedom,
wide windows, your heart,
fists raised high in a column
holding up the sky.

You went up to night's silent bed
with star crystals in your hair,
a contemporary saint, a revolutionary.
I saw you that last day
as a living planet,
full of ideas, shining with life
spinning round me and round us up there.

Tus manos dieron luz, Erich Fried,
y tus ojos juventud.
Chile sentirá tu silencio
cuando se libre del fascismo,
entonces la voz de Chile, Erich Fried,
Nicaragua y Palestina,
te llamará a los cielos,
buscándote por el mundo
con el grito ¡Libertad!

Your hands gave light, Erich Fried
and your eyes gave youth.
Chile will feel your silence
when she is rid of fascism,
then Erich Fried, the voices of Chile,
Nicaragua, Palestine
will be calling for you to come
back down to our earth
crying: We need
Freedom!

D.L.

LA PRIMAVERA DE MICHAEL DOLAN

Una lluvia rota por el tiempo
empapará las desoladas colinas de Escocia
y una gaita apretará la noche en un lamento
el quebranto de tu ausencia Michael Dolan.
Otra lágrima de luna callará
el brillo de tu alma en la flor de la higuera
y una mujer cantará a capela
tu pena al eco del silencio;
y llegó el Primero de Mayo
sin anuncio del calendario,
anónimo a los ojos que miran por la ventana
las falsas horas que cierran el día;
tan distinta explosión de pétalos de colores
que solo tú comprendiste su sensible mutación,
las manos que abrazan la forma
de la luz y de la sombra;
de tal modo el mutismo de los apacibles ríos
que serpenteaban versátiles en el paisaje,
se desbordaron torrentes
sin caudal que los contenga,
corazón que se deshiela
después de largo invernar bajo la niebla.
Atrás queda diminuta la razón
tal trofeo de guerra hundido en un sendero vaporoso
y la vida suspendida
a un accidente de una nota de jazz.

MICHAEL DOLAN'S SPRING

Rain shall soak the desolate hills of Scotland
and bagpipes in the night lament you, Michael Dolan.
Moontears tarnish your soulshine
to a figtree flower
and a woman sings your pain
a capella to the echo of silence.
Came the first of May
the calendar didn't announce it,
it was nameless
to those who looked through the window
at the treacherous hours which closed that day;
such a distinct explosion of coloured petals
that only you understood the whirling emotions,
hands which cupped the shape of light and dark;
and the tranquillity of rivers
winding their ways through the country
became flooding torrents
no banks could contain,
heart melting after the long foggy winter
reason diminished and jettisoned
like warspoils on a difficult path
and life suspended
on a jazz accidental.

Cual bellísima perversa rosa
clavó sus auras en tu soledad,
dramático lenguaje que te dejó yerto.
Porque las flores son esculturas de la luz,
pitonisas colmadas de pasión
que podemos husmear hasta quedar ebrios
por el bálsamo de sus sentimientos.
Porque solo dolor y ausencia
sopla el viento vestido de salmos,
entonces queda nada más que soledad.

A beautiful sick rose
nailed its sweetness to your loneliness,
rhetoric which left you cold.
Because flowers are light sculptures,
passionate pythonesses,
their balm can intoxicate.
Because only pain and absence
blows on the psalm-clothed wind,
then nothing but solitude.

D.L.

ANUNCIACION

Si te contara
los secretos de mis sueños,
aves en presagio vuelo
alto sobre los cielos,
anunciarían mal tiempo en el sur
destino hacia el norte,
y las nubes tempestuosas apretan
la lluvia al corazón.

Alusión a que no estamos aquí
ni la luna naciendo del lago.

Ahora lejos del abrigo de los cisnes
entiendo mi por qué:
ausente tersura de amapolas,
maltrecha nave de naufragios.

Morado velo melancolía
colgué en Las Cruces,
tantas estrellas idas
con nuestros ojos
perdidos en la noche.
Agonía en la boca del pescado
y cenizas de todo tiempo
flotando en el vacío.

ANNUNCIATION

I could tell you
my secrets dreams
birds flying high portending
bad weather in the south
moving northwards
and storm clouds raining
rain in my heart

Meaning
we are neither at home here
nor we can see the moon
rising out of the lake.

Far now from protecting swans
I understand what I am:
an absence of shining popies,
a battered shipwreck.

I hung a veil of sadness
violet over Las Cruces
where so many stars had died
and the light in our eyes went out.
Agony in the fish's mouth
and all time's ashes
floating in space.

Olas insaciables
destemplan sentimientos,
campanas que replican en la playa.
Dragones azules
al confín de tus entrañas,
rompieron el cristal de tu estalactita.

Yo no hice penitencias de suplicios
ni escondí de mi boca amarga espuma.

Sí para amarte debo morir,
aquí te devuelvo los lirios blancos
en reverso a tu desafío:
para amarte voy a vivir.

Insatiable waves stir feelings,
on the beach bells ring.
We were blue dragons
diving deep into you
shattering your crystal sheen.

And neither did I repent
nor spit bitter regret.

If to love you I must die
I'll give you back your white lilies
and give back your challenge:
to love you I shall live.

D.L.